Heart cries to heaven

A Book of Prayers

heat
cries to
heaven

The Quest for Character 3

David Campbell
Compiled by Sara Leone

DayOne

© Day One Publications 2010
First Edition 2010

Unless otherwise indicated, Scripture quotations in this publication are from The New International Version, copyright ©1973, 1978, 1984, International Bible Society. Used by permission of Hodder and Stoughton, a member of the Hodder Headline Group. All rights reserved.

British Library Cataloguing in Publication Data available

ISBN 978-1-84625-229-7

Published by Day One Publications
Ryelands Road, Leominster, HR6 8NZ

☎ 01568 613 740
FAX: 01568 611 473
email—sales@dayone.co.uk
web site—www.dayone.co.uk

Designed by Wayne McMaster and printed by Thomson Litho, East Kilbride

Contents

4

Prayers of Invocation and Adoration

Praise for our Saviour

Hebrews 7:25
'Therefore he
is able to save
completely
those who
come to God
through him,
because he
always lives to
intercede for
them.'

Our Father in heaven,
We thank you for a Saviour who is fully equal to
all of the demands of saving sinners,

> for One whose blood has perfectly atoned for
> human sin,
> for One whose righteousness covers all our sin,
> and for One whose mighty Spirit is able to bring
> us from death to life,
> and from life in Christ here on earth to fulness of
> life in your presence.

Lord, you know how often men fail us.
We look to them to help us in some respect, and they are
either unable or unwilling,

> but we thank you that it is not so when it comes to
> the most crucial of all issues
> —how we can be right with you.

We thank you for a Saviour who is both able and willing
to save all who come to you by him.

We thank you for the strength of his commitment to
every one of his blood-bought people,

> for his commitment to continuing the work that
> he has begun in us,
> to protecting us from the world, the flesh, and the
> devil;
> and from all those forces ranged against us which
> have such power to destroy us if we were left to
> ourselves.

We pray that we, who are your people today, would be
comforted in the knowledge of whose hands we have
placed our eternal concerns, that being in the hands of
Jesus we can be in no better place.

Those who trust in him will never be put to shame.

We pray that your blessing, O God, this day would
be on the preaching of Christ, that many others
> would be sovereignly drawn to put their trust
> in him,
> would enter into that living, loving, lasting
> union,
> and would know the blessedness of being
> joined to that love from which nothing can
> ever separate us.
>> Come to us, we pray, O God;
>> Come in Christ,
>> Come by the Spirit, and richly bless us.

We pray that we may be able to leave all our cares
and concerns with you.
Give us grace to cast every one of them upon you,
including the burden of our sin, for the blood of
Jesus Christ cleanses from all sin.
> We would confess our sin;
> We would receive his forgiveness;
> We would open our hearts wide to all of the
> influences of grace this day.
We pray that you will come down, O Lord, as
dew upon the dry ground, as sunshine, with every
spiritual refreshment.

Grant to us humble and teachable hearts that
there may be a deep receptiveness to all that you
have to say.
> May we be comforted;
> May we have grace to give you the glory and
> the praise that are your due.

Help us, we pray, for Jesus' sake.
Amen.

Praise to the One Living and True God

Psalm
22:27–28
'All the ends
of the earth
will remember
and turn to the
Lord, and all
the families
of the nations
will bow down
before him,
for dominion
belongs to the
Lord and he
rules over the
nations.'

Almighty God,
  You are the only One to be worshipped,
  For you are the one living and true God.
  You are to be loved with all our heart and soul
  and strength and mind;
  You alone are to be served.

We pray that you will be merciful to the multitudes upon multitudes of our fellow human beings who worship other gods.

Your Word declares those gods to be false gods; indeed it declares them to be nothing, and yet we know that behind them there are demonic powers at work that hold the worshippers in their grip.

You know the blindness that is over so many minds, and the degrading superstitions to which these demonic powers have reduced so many of our fellow men.
  They call upon a god who cannot hear;
  They put their trust in a god who cannot save.
  Have mercy upon them, we pray.

You are the great God, the King over all gods; you are mightier than all those demonic powers who hold so many in darkness, and you are able to deliver them and to make them true worshippers.

We pray that by the power of the Holy Spirit, through the gospel that is preached today, miracles of grace would take place in vast numbers, and that those who have worshipped other gods would come to bow before you, to worship and serve you alone, for you are worthy.

We pray that we,

      Who have the privilege of knowing you,

      And of being the sheep of your pasture,

      The flock under your care,

          may sense how great is our privilege;

      May we have grace to delight in you,

      May we be confident in you as the God who has taken us for his own.

      May we worship you not just with our lips, but with our hearts and with our lives.

May we demonstrate not only in this building, but in the very way that we live our lives in our homes, and in our places of work,

      That you really are our God,

      That we are your people,

      And that we are living through Christ in obedience to you.

Hear us at the outset of this hour of worship.

      We thank you for this day,

      We thank you for one another,

      We thank you for this building in which we meet,

      And we thank you for Jesus our Saviour,

      The Mediator between God and man,

      The great Bridge that has bridged over the gulf our sin has created and has brought us to you.

Bless us while we worship for our Saviour's sake.
Amen.

The Lord is Good

Psalm 34:8–10
'Taste and see
that the LORD is
good. Blessed
is the man who
takes refuge in
him.
Fear the LORD,
you his saints,
for those who
fear him lack
nothing.
The lions may
grow weak and
hungry, but
those who seek
the LORD lack
no good thing.'

Lord, so many of us have tasted and experienced for
ourselves just how good you are because you have
heard our cries for mercy.

>You have delivered us from evil;
>You have saved so many of us from our sins.
>We know you as the God who is good to
>undeserving sinners, the God who is good
>continually to his beloved people.

We know that in a broad sense, we have all, regardless
of our spiritual state, experienced so much of your
goodness, but we do ask that those of us who know you
as good to us in Christ would drink more deeply of that
goodness today as you, through him, pour into our lives
further spiritual blessing, and we pray that there may be
others who would taste of that goodness for the first time
today.

May they come to know you as God in Christ
>Who reaches out to the lost,
>Who through the cross has provided for our
>salvation,
>And who now invites us to come to your beloved
>Son that in him we might be justified.

Do draw near to us, our gracious, good, and loving God;
>Bless us with your presence,
>And the work of the Spirit in our hearts to stir us
>up to worship you with fervency and joy
>and to give us humble and teachable hearts that
>we might receive believingly and obediently your
>Word.

Forgive us, we pray, for our sins.
Cleanse us through Jesus' blood from all
unrighteousness.

      And give us grace to glory in you.

Through Jesus we pray.
Amen.

Prayer for Saving Blessing

O ur great and gracious God,
  We thank you that there is a cross in human
  history, a cross on which your beloved Son died,
  the Lamb of God who takes away the sin of the
  world.

We could not have made ourselves right with you;
We would have been eternally ruined, were it not for that
cross.
> We thank you for the blood that was shed,
> The blood that cleanses from all sin.

But we thank you that there is more than a cross—
> That there is an empty tomb,
> And that on the third day our crucified Saviour
> rose to life again,
>> Afterwards ascended into heaven,
>> And is now exalted at your right hand—
>> The One who is upon the throne!

With the angels and with the spirits of just men made
perfect, and the whole church of Christ on earth,
> We would worship him,
> The Lamb who was slain,
> But who now lives to pour out his blessing upon
> those for whom he died.

We pray, Lord Jesus, that this day you would be
appropriately worshipped,
And we pray that from heaven,
> Your dwelling place,
> And from your almighty, gracious, heavenly
> throne,

Horatius Bonar, 1866
'Blessing and honour and glory and power, Wisdom and riches and strength evermore Give ye to him who our battle hath won, Whose are the kingdom, the crown, and the throne.'

It would please you to pour out saving blessing
here and all around the world.

We ask it for your eternal glory,
For the glory of the Father who sent you,
And for the glory of the Spirit who brings these
things to life to us and makes us yours.
Amen.

Prayer for Gospel Light

Psalm 34:17
'The righteous
cry out, and
the LORD
hears them; he
delivers them
from all their
troubles.'

Lord, with grateful hearts we approach you, the living
God, the glorious God.
How merciful you have been to us
> In giving us a revelation of yourself,
> In drawing near to us,
> In not giving us up to the worship of false gods,
>> gods of wood or stone,
>> gods who are nothing more than a figment
>> of our imagination.

You have brought us face to face with yourself, Almighty
God, the Creator of the heavens and the earth, and
the gracious covenant God who in mercy to his people
provided atonement for our sins that we might know
you, love you, and ultimately dwell in your presence for
evermore.

You are the God who hears his people's prayers; how
many of us can identify with the psalmist and those of
whom he speaks in their cries to you in fear and in need.
> You have heard;
> You have delivered;
> And you have protected.

Afresh this morning and throughout this day,
> We would taste and see that the Lord is good.
> We would repose our confidence in you once
> again and in the truth of your holy Word.

We pray that you will draw near to us as we wait upon
you in this hour.

We ask for your blessing upon those who are unable to
be with us today.

14

We remember those who are upon our hearts and for whom we are especially burdened.

> Hear our prayers for them.

We ask you to bless the ministries of our church. Thank you for the freedom that we have to reach out in so many different ways with the gospel and with means to build up your people.

> Remember our missionaries serving you in different parts of the world.
> Remember your persecuted people in different parts of the world,
>> and throw around them the shield and arms of your protection; keep them in your peace.

Lord, be merciful to our world in all its terrible darkness and sin.

We ask that you will continue to send forth the light. May that light of the gospel of our Lord Jesus Christ illumine this very day the hearts of multitudes throughout our world.

May our Lord Jesus Christ see much of the travail of his soul this day and be satisfied.

Come to us, we pray, in each part of our worship.

> Thank you for the privilege of singing the great hymns and psalms of our faith.
> Thank you for the Word of God that is to be read, and for the exposition of that Word.

Lord, for these and for all your good gifts we give you thanks.

We implore your blessing through Jesus Christ our Lord. Amen.

Praise for Christ, our Great High Priest

Hebrews 7:27b
'He sacrificed for their sins once for all when he offered himself.'

Our great and gracious God,
   We thank you for the ministry of our Lord Jesus Christ, our great High Priest.
We thank you for his priestly work on earth.
We glory in One who was both offering and offerer,

> for the Son of God who loved us and gave himself for us, and for that perfect atonement of the cross of Calvary.

We thank you for his high priestly work on our behalf at this time,

> for his intercession for us,
> and for the way in which you always hear his prayers as he prays to you for those who come to you by him.

Lord, we would not seek to add anything to that sacrifice;

> We dare not—it is finished,
> And we glory in it as finished and in the perfection of his high priestly work both on earth and in heaven.

We would commit ourselves unreservedly to him to be saved by him, and we would never move from the footing of grace on which we have come to stand at the outset of our Christian lives.

We worship him, O God, as the Saviour of the world, the One who, by his death, purchased men for God from every nation, tribe, people, and tongue.

We are so grateful to you that the gospel is not just for

16

the few, not just for the one nation, but for all nations.

   We ourselves have been the recipients of that
   blessing for the world.
   We thank you for the gospel that has come to us,
   for the power with which it has come to so many
   of us here; we have believed, and Jesus Christ has
   become our Saviour.
   We would unitedly, with all our hearts, cry to you
   for the world—
         for the nations, for the multitudes that are
         still in darkness.
   O God, shine your light upon them, shine with the
   gospel, and shine into their hearts that they might
   turn to the Saviour, believe, and be saved.
         We know that this is the greatest thing that
         our world needs.

We pray for peace, and we pray for plenty where there is
famine,
We pray for places where there is violence and bloodshed
that that would cease, but we know that it is the gospel
that is needed above everything else, and we pray that
you will send forth the gospel.

         Lord, here we are and we have that gospel;
         We have the Bible in our own language and we
         have the privilege, for many of us, of hearing it in
         our homes, we hear it in our churches, and we will
         hear it again this day.

We pray that you will give us grace.
May no one here have a hardened heart against such a
gracious God who once again would freely offer Jesus
Christ and righteousness in him to them.

         We pray that your Spirit would be at work even
         as your Word is preached, and that those who
         are without righteousness, would, like Abraham,
         come to believe, so that righteousness may be

17

credited to them.

We pray, O God, that you would attend your Word with power that it may effect great and lasting change.

> Overshadow us, we pray, with your Spirit.
> Come and visit every heart.
> Give us grace to put aside all other cares and to give ourselves wholly to the Word that is before us now.
> We pray that it will be blessed to every heart.

We ask it through Jesus Christ our Lord.
Amen.

Prayer for God's Presence in Worship

Lord,
We pray for churches known to us, and many
that are unknown, that are looking to you for the
provision of pastoral leadership;
We pray, Lord Jesus, that you, who give pastors
and teachers, would give those gifts to the
churches where they are needed,

> that the work of the Kingdom would
> continue, and that your people would
> be built up and equipped for the works
> of service, and protected through the
> faithful teaching, preaching and leadership
> of godly pastors from all the unsound
> doctrine that they are ever exposed to.

We pray for your blessing upon your churches
and ask, Lord, that they may flourish.

Grant, God, we pray, that this day would be
profitable to us, and profitable for all the people
of God all over the world.

> You have given us this day,
> You have given us your Word,
> And you have given us the Spirit.

We pray that in and through all of these things, you may
meet with us.
Build us up in our faith and build and extend the church

For your everlasting praise and glory,
Amen.

Thomas Benson Pollock, 1871
'Jesus, with thy church abide,
Be her Saviour,
Lord, and Guide,
While on earth her faith is tried:
We beseech thee, hear us.'

Praise to God of Forgiving Love

Micah 7:18–19
'Who is a God like you, who pardons sin and forgives the transgression of the remnant of his inheritance? You do not stay angry for ever but delight to show mercy. You will again have compassion on us; you will tread our sins underfoot and hurl all our iniquities into the depths of the sea.'

Lord, what an amazing thing it is that we human beings, the human race that has so offended and grieved you, should yet have in you a God who is ever so ready to pardon.

What a marvellous thing it is that if we will but turn from our sins and seek your face and implore your forgiveness, you will forgive!
> Though our sins should be of the very worst kind and multiplied beyond number,
> Yet you will take those sins,
>> tread them underfoot,
>> and hurl them into the depths of the seas.

We thank you for the experience that so many of us have had of this gracious forgiveness,
And we thank you for the ongoing experience that we have had of it as, day after day, we have come to you with fresh sin, and when confessed, you have forgiven.
> We would worship you, the gracious God,
>> who, through the cross of Calvary,
>> made provision for our cleansing.

We would ask that at the outset of our worship there would be in our hearts lifted to you,
> Confession,
> Repentance,
> The imploring of your forgiveness,
> And the experience again through Jesus' blood of the washing away of our guilt.

20

Grant it so that we may come in the joy of reconciliation,
in the joy of fresh forgiveness,
in the joy of knowing that you are a God who now
through Christ smiles upon us in forgiving love.
Hear us and bless this hour of worship.

We pray it in Jesus' name.
Amen.

Praise To the Covenant-Keeping God

Genesis 12:3b
' ... all peoples on earth will be blessed through you.'

Our great and gracious God,
We thank you for the fulfilment of the promise
made so long ago to Abraham
And we thank you for his offspring through
whom all nations on earth have been, and will
continue to be, blessed.

We see in that promise the promise of our Lord Jesus
Christ, and we thank you for One through whom you are
blessing the world
—the One who when he was upon the cross of
Calvary—
purchased men for God from every nation, tribe,
people, and tongue.

We thank you for the Great Commission to go and make
disciples of all the nations
And we thank you that we ourselves have come to believe
—so many of us—
in this promised Saviour.

We thank you for his power at work in our hearts and for
the creation of a godly fear.
We would manifest that fear as Abraham did, in a
life of obedience.
Help us, we pray, to walk in your ways
And to manifest thereby the change that you have
wrought in us by your mighty grace.

Lord, we live in a world where one of its dark features is
that there is no fear of God before the eyes of humanity
in general.
We live in a society where we see the evidences of

that on every hand.

We pray that your blessing would be upon the proclamation of the gospel,

      the proclamation of Jesus Christ,

            that, to those who have no fear of God, the gospel would come,

            and would come with conviction,

            and with regenerating power

      to make those men and women, boys and girls, to truly fear and love you.

Hear us for Jesus' sake.

Amen.

Praise to Jesus, the King of Kings

Luke 1:33
'... and he will reign over the house of Jacob for ever; his kingdom will never end.'

Lord Jesus Christ, we worship you as the King, the One who in fulfilment of promise, are reigning over the house of Jacob and of whose kingdom there is no end.

> What a great and glorious King you are!
> You have no equal;
> There is nothing that is not under your almighty sway.
> You are King of kings and Lord of lords,
> You are the Ruler over all nature;
>> All demons are subject to you,
>> You have the hearts of all men in your hands,
>> You determine our destinies,
>> You have the whole world under your government.

We thank you especially for that reign of grace that you have established in the hearts and lives of your people.

> We were captives,
> We were bound,
> We could not break free,
> And you came in kingly power and mighty grace,
>> You delivered us from the power of sin,
>> From the power of Satan,
>> And you now reign in their place.

We who are your people are so glad that the King of the universe is the King over our hearts and lives.

> We, your people, would be loyal and devoted servants of such a King.
> We desire for the coming of your kingdom with

24

ever increasing power
>in our own lives,
>in the lives of others,
>and in the world as a whole.

To that end, we pray, Lord Jesus, that it would please you to establish your kingdom in the hearts of needy sinners today in great numbers.

>Be merciful to those here, we pray, who are still in the grip of sin, over whom Satan still has such power. We ask that you will come to them as you have come to us;
>>break the chains that bind them,
>>deliver them,
>>and bring them under your own sweet and gracious government.

We pray not only for those here who are in need of your grace, but multitudes all around the world; for we desire that the One who is rightfully King, and the One who is truly reigning would come to be worshipped and adored as such, and to have his rightful place in multitudes upon multitudes of his fellow human beings.

Heavenly Father, glorify your Son, we pray.
Send the Holy Spirit that men and women, boys and girls, may love him and live for him all their days.

>>We thank you for the assurance of his presence, for where two or three are present in his name, he has said that he will be present;

We would receive that by faith.

>>We would bless you that you are here, Lord Jesus,

>Though we cannot see you with our own eyes;
>>You are here in all the fulness of your power,
>>in the greatness of your love,

and in the perfection of your knowledge of
our hearts and lives,
our circumstances and our needs.

We pray that it would please you to minister to us as you
see we have need, and so work in us that we in turn
may believe in you,
submit to you,
thank you,
and glorify you
for the great God, King, and Saviour that
you are.

Thank you for the kind providence that has brought us
together today.

Thank you for the Lord's Day and for all that it means
to us.

Bless this hour and the day as a whole, for your glory's
sake we ask it.
Amen.

Praise for the Holy Spirit

Our Father in heaven,
We give you thanks for the promise of the Spirit and
We thank you for the fulfilment of that promise in the experience of every believer.

We cannot see the Spirit.
He is invisible God and yet your Word assures us that at the moment we believed in Christ, he came and took up residence in our hearts.

We thank you that there he remains—an ever-living presence—

to sanctify us,
to give us grace to press on in the Christian life,
and to equip and empower us for Christian service.

We thank you for all that we have known of his blessed ministry, and we thank you for all that we shall know as he continues to work in us until the work is complete.

We thank you that his presence in the world is not merely to live in the hearts of the Lord's people;
It is to come and to bring the Word of the gospel to bear upon the hearts and lives of those who are not yet believers.

We thank you for his ministry in regeneration—for the way in which he breathes new life into those who are dead in their transgressions and sins.

We pray that all over the world today,
and here in this building, the Spirit would be at work,

Galatians 3:14
'He redeemed us in order that the blessing given to Abraham might come to the Gentiles through Christ Jesus, so that by faith we might receive the promise of the Spirit.'

bringing conviction of sin,
opening the eyes of unbelievers,
persuading them and enabling
them to embrace Jesus Christ freely
offered to them in the gospel.

We pray that the Spirit would take of the things of
Christ and make them known to us this day.
We pray that we may enjoy his illuminating
ministry
and that what we see, through the
Scriptures, the things he shows to us—

We pray that they may move us deeply,
and may warm our hearts towards you,
our gracious God in heaven.
May they prompt us to obedience;
May they stir our hearts to greater
thankfulness, love, and praise, and
a deeper dedication of ourselves to
you and to your service.

May your blessing be upon this hour of worship.
May your blessing be upon this whole day.
We pray that it would be a most blessed day for everyone
here,
for the church throughout the world,
and for multitudes who, even at this moment, are
still in the darkness and bondage of sin.

Come, O God, we pray, the God who has so manifested
his power and presence,
his glory and grace,
on this most special of days.

All over the world, make it a day ever to be remembered through all eternity as the day when multitudes met with Christ and came into a living, loving, lasting union with him.

We ask these things in his name and for his glory.
Amen.

Prayer for Increased Grace through the Word

Psalm 84:2
'*My soul yearns, even faints, for the courts of the* LORD; *my heart and my flesh cry out for the living God.*'

Our great God in heaven,
We thank you for the grace that has implanted in the hearts of your people a desire after you.
We hunger and thirst for you, the living God.

Our heart and flesh cry out for you.
We can never be satisfied unless you come
and we are privileged to have communion with you.
We pray that you will draw near to us,
and fulfill those desires that you yourself have implanted.

We pray that when we come to the Word
it will be your voice that we hear.
We pray the Spirit will take what is read and what is preached, and implant it deep within our hearts.
We pray that it will be a Word that brings us nearer to you.
We pray that it will also be a Word that you will use to bring those who are not yet saved,
to know you as their own God and Saviour.

We know that there are some here, and that there are multitudes throughout our world, who do not have this heart longing after you, and we pray for them.
We pray that you will open their eyes that they may see that
you are the altogether lovely One
—ever to be desired—
that their hearts may go out after you,
that they may long to be reconciled to you,

and will seek you and, in your mercy,
find you.

We give you thanks for the privileges that are ours this
day to serve you in different ways and we do commit to
you the various activities of this day.

We thank you for the fellowship that we are able to enjoy
together.

Through Jesus Christ we pray these things.
Amen.

Praise to the God who is Light

Heavenly Father,
We thank you that by your grace towards those
of us who are your children, we have come to love
holiness.
We delight in it when we see it in your people.

There is to us no lovelier person in all the world
than the one whom you have made holy, and with
the psalmist we can say,

> 'As for the saints who are in the land,
> they are the glorious ones in whom is all
> my delight.'

Above all we delight in holiness as we see it in you.
> We worship you as the God who is light, in
> whom there is no darkness at all.
> We are full of sin;
> We are stained,
But you are altogether beautiful,
You are perfect, and in you there is no flaw
whatsoever.

We thank you for your purpose in grace towards your
people to make us holy, like you, and we pray that you
will send the Holy Spirit into our midst and into our
hearts this day to continue that work—to begin it in the
lives of those who are still strangers to your grace, and to
carry us on, we who are your people, to a greater likeness
to yourself.

As you do so, as we meet in your presence,

*Charles
Wesley, 1740*
*'Just and holy
is thy Name, I
am all unright-
eousness;
False and full
of sin I am;
thou art full
of truth and
grace.'*

And as you meet with us,
We pray that you would stir up our hearts to
thankfulness and to worship of you, our great and
holy God.

Through Jesus Christ we pray these things.
Amen.

Christmas Prayers of Thanks

Luke 2:10–11

'But the angel said to them, "Do not be afraid. I bring you good news of great joy that will be for all the people. Today in the town of David a Saviour has been born to you; he is Christ the Lord."'

Our gracious God in heaven,
We would bow in humility and in adoration.
You so loved the world that you gave your one
and only Son.
We thank you for the inspired record that we have of
the announcement of his birth and of the birth itself.
We thank you that One

> who had been anticipated for centuries,
> who had been repeatedly promised,
> was, at last, given and sent.

We rejoice in the good news that his birth is not
only for the people of Israel, but for the world as
a whole.
We rejoice in One who is not merely man but God.
We would worship you, Lord Jesus,

> as God manifest in flesh,
> as the God who became flesh and you
> made your dwelling among us,
> so that we who were poor might, by your
> grace, become rich.

We thank you that you are a King, and though so
many in our world today do not recognize you as
a King, you are a King.

> You are upon a throne this day,
> and we worship you as the One who rules
> over all
> and who in a very special way rules in the
> hearts of your people.

We pray that this day it would please you to so
work in the hearts of multitudes throughout this
world, that they would come to know you

34

as the King,
as the Lord,
as the Saviour, whom you were sent to be.

We rejoice, Lord, that this day, in fulfilment of
the prayers of many, there will be many who will
come to know you as their own King and Lord
and Saviour.
We pray that there would be some here.

Enable us, we pray, to look beyond what was
merely apparent to the human eye,
to discern your true identity,
the wonder of this event,
the great issues that hung upon it,
the work that it brought you into the world
to do,
the triumph of our Saviour through the
cross,
and the eternal life that now comes to
everyone who believes in you.

We would gladly join with angels and with the saints
throughout the world, and we would adore you.

We pray that, by your grace, we would do so
throughout this hour of worship, and throughout
this day,
throughout these coming weeks and months,
and indeed, all through our lives.

Bless us and be with us by your Spirit;
Open our eyes that we may see you in all your
greatness and glory.

We ask it for your great name's sake.
Amen.

Joy to the World

Isaac Watts, 1719

'Joy to the world! the Lord is come: Let earth receive her King; Let every heart prepare him room, And heav'n and nature sing.'

O ur great and gracious God,
We thank you for One who came
'to make his blessings flow, far as the curse is found.'

> And you know, and we know, how far that curse is found;
> it is universal.

It is not only a curse upon the ground on account of our sins; we ourselves are under the curse. Your Word tells us so plainly that cursed is everyone who does not continue in everything that the law demands.
We have all failed to do everything that your law demands.
We stand before that law convicted of having broken it,
> and are exposed justly to your great displeasure.

But we thank you that One has come, our Lord Jesus Christ,

> to redeem us from the curse of the law,
> to deliver us from that condemnation that we had brought upon ourselves by our sin.

Lord, truly this is 'joy to the world', and we pray that it would be heard as such.

> It is joy to us,
>> and we pray that so it would be heard by us,
>> and that we would give you thanks this Christmas season with all our hearts for One who came to deliver us from sin and from judgement.

We thank you for the opportunity that we will have, and many others besides, to proclaim again the coming of our Lord Jesus Christ, the fulfilment of ancient promise.

> We pray that you will bless that proclamation;
> We ask that you will bless the services today;
> We thank you that you have brought us together;
> We thank you for one another;
> And we pray for your rich blessing to be upon us
> as we unite together for Christian worship.

Draw near to us we pray. Make Christ real and precious to us, for his name's sake.
Amen.

An Invocation at Year's End

Samuel Medley, 1738–1799 'God shall alone the refuge be, And comfort of my mind; Too wise to be mistaken, He, Too good to be unkind.'

How we thank you, our gracious God,
   that we can look up from the circumstances that
   surround us,
   and that are often so painful and perplexing,
   and we can turn our eyes upon you, the God with
   our times in your hand.

We rejoice and take comfort in the knowledge that
ultimately you are the One who rules over all, and who is
determining what takes place in our lives.
      We would be comforted in the knowledge that at
      the helm is a God who is infinitely wise, and most
      loving—
            a God who is too wise to be mistaken,
            too good to be unkind.

We pray that as we face the unknown days of this year
that is so soon to begin, we would do so with the peace
that comes from knowing that
      you will be with us,
      you will uphold us,
      you will rule over all things,
      and make them work together for our good.

We thank you for this hour of worship and pray that you
will draw near to each one of us.
      Help us as we sing your praise;
      Give to us tender and receptive spirits, that we may
      hear your voice speaking to the very depths of our
      spirit. Hear us, and take glory to yourself through
            our praise,
            our faith,
            and our obedience.

We ask it through Jesus Christ our Lord.
Amen.

Prayers of
Confession

Prayer for Forgiveness

Count Nikolaus Ludwig von Zinzendorf, 1739 Translated by John Wesley, 1740, alt.

Lord, your Word is so honest with us,
   So emphatic in its declaration that by our
   observance of your law there is no one who can be
   justified in your sight;
   Rather it is through the law that we become
   conscious of our sin.

It is like a mirror,
   And when we look into that mirror, we see our
   faults.
   The more closely we study it, the more our faults
   appear.

The law condemns us, and it offers us no forgiveness.
   It confronts us with our sin,
   But has nothing to say about pardon and
   justification.

But we thank you that in your great mercy you have not
left us in the hands of the law.
   We thank you that alongside of it there is a
   Redeemer,
   One who, knowing the full extent of our guilt,
   took it all upon himself,
      that he might atone for it by his precious
      blood.

We thank you that because his amazing sacrifice,
   we, who stand condemned before the law,
   can be forgiven,
   can have our stains wholly washed out,
   can come to be clothed in a righteousness
   not of own but from Christ himself
   —his own righteousness—

'Jesus, be endless praise to thee, Whose boundless mercy hath for me — For me a full atonement made, An everlasting ransom paid.'

and in him we can come to stand before
you faultless.

We thank you that through faith in him that
righteousness and forgiveness become ours.

Thank you that so many of us here have come to know
you as the God of salvation, the God who, through the
cross, has put us into a right relationship with himself.

We pray for others here who have not yet come to
Calvary and to the Son of God.
>May they have grace to do so even this day,
>and may those of your people who,
>notwithstanding your great goodness, have
>sinned, again find fresh forgiveness through the
>same blood of Jesus Christ.

For our Saviour's sake, we pray.
Amen.

Prayer for Light in a Dark and Fallen World

Romans 3:23
'... for all have sinned and fall short of the glory of God.'

Lord, we confess that we are part of a fallen world.
We stand chargeable with sin along with every other human being,
And we know that things in that regard are no different today than they were when the Apostle wrote his letter to the Romans.

But we thank you, most gracious God, that into this scene of darkness and rebellion, and in the very midst of so many expressions of your righteous wrath, there came Jesus and with him the good news of a righteousness from God.

We thank you for that righteousness and for the good news that proclaims it to others and offers it freely to all.
We would by faith take hold of that righteousness ourselves that we too might be justified.
We pray that all over the world today in the darkest places
the light of the gospel would shine
and would bring not only intellectual understanding of the truth,
but a heartfelt experience of that truth.

Almighty God, we ask that you will work on a massive scale today, drawing thousands and tens of thousands into the kingdom.
We know that you are able,
And we pray that for your glory's sake you will do it.

Through Jesus Christ, our Lord, we ask these things.
Amen.

Prayer of Confession before the Lord's Supper

Horatius Bonar, 1843

'I lay my sins on Jesus, the spotless Lamb of God; He bears them all, and frees us from the accursed load: I bring my guilt to Jesus, to wash my crimson stains White in his blood most precious, till not a spot remains.'

All-seeing, holy, righteous God, the God who knows and hates our sin,

We would humble ourselves before you.

We would not in the pride of our hearts strut before you, congratulating ourselves on our own endeavours to keep the law of God and to please you.

We have sinned.

We confess that to you.

In our hearts and in our lives we would exercise repentance,

we would turn from all that is hateful to you,

and we would pray that every sin that you, the all-seeing God, detect, it would please you to blot out.

Create in us a clean heart, we pray; renew in us a right spirit.

Against you, you only, have we sinned.

Blot out all our transgressions

And restore to your people the joy of our salvation.

How we thank you that we can come and make such petitions on behalf of ourselves knowing that though you are so awesomely holy, and in righteousness abhor all that is sinful, yet you are a most gracious and merciful God. You love the sinner, and you love when the sinner cries from the depths and confesses his sin.

Gracious, righteous God,

you have provided in the cross of Calvary for our
cleansing,
for our renewal,
and our ultimate perfection.
We thank you for the love that moved you to give your
Son to the death of the cross.

We thank you, Son of God, for loving us and giving
yourself for us, and for the promise that your blood is
able to cleanse from all sin.
We would enjoy that cleansing and that renewal,
And we pray that your Spirit, O God, would be
mightily operative in the hearts of your people,
subduing sin,
transforming us into the likeness of Jesus
Christ.
We thank you that that is your purpose in
predestination.

You have foreknown us, called us, and justified us, that
we might be conformed to the likeness of Jesus Christ;
and we thank you that, having begun a good work in us,
you will carry it on until it is complete.

We pray that you will use this gathering,
The means of grace, the hymns and psalms that
we sing,
The Scriptures read and studied,
And the ordinance of the Lord's Supper
to help us heavenward,
to work in us holiness,
to deepen our love for you,
our gratitude for your grace,
and our abhorrence of all that is sinful.
Lord, put your finger, we pray, upon our sins if we

are blind to them.
Search us, O God, and know our hearts;
      see if there is any sinful way in us, and
      point us in the way everlasting.

Lord, as we experience the blessings of redemption,
      We pray that all over the world today those same
      blessings would be enjoyed.
      May they be experienced by those who have never
      tasted of your goodness in salvation before.
      May be they be experienced again by your own
      beloved people who have sinned and who need
      once again to be forgiven.

      We thank you again for this time together.
      We seek most earnestly your blessing to be upon
      us as we join together.
      We pray that this would be indeed for our
      spiritual benefit
            but we pray that supremely it would be for
            the glory, praise, and pleasure of our great
            triune God—Father, Son, and Holy Spirit.
Amen.

Communion Prayer

Most holy God,
We bow humbly in your presence.
We thank you for an atonement through which
our sins of irreverence can be forgiven.

Forgive us whenever in our behaviour and our worship
we have failed to see
What a great and awesome and holy God you are.
And how marvellous that we can anticipate
—for the Scriptures assure us we can anticipate—
being presented before the presence of your glory
with exceeding joy.
How marvellous!
How wonderful the perfection of Christ's
atoning work!

We pray that,
As we come to this table, it may be with renewed
thankfulness for this offering by which the unholy
are made holy, and ultimately fitted for the
unveiled presence of God.

Lord, we pray for those here who are in their sins this day
and are wholly unfit for your presence.
Let them not imagine, O God, that just as they are
it will be all well with them.
We pray that you will bring them face to face with
the revelation of yourself,
that they may see how great is their need of
the atoning sacrifice of Jesus.

Jude 24–25
*'To him who
is able to keep
you from
falling and
to present
you before
his glorious
presence
without fault
and with great
joy—to the
only God our
Saviour be
glory, majesty,
power and
authority,
through Jesus
Christ our
Lord,
before all ages,
now and for
evermore!
Amen.'*

Call them, we pray, by your grace.
Surprise your burdened and sorrowing people
with joy as their loved ones, those who cannot
come and sit at the table, may one day be able
to join with the family of God, remembering the
Christ who has died for them, and who has saved
them from their sins.

Hear us, we pray, for Jesus' sake.
Amen.

Thanksgiving for the Table of Remembrance

Horatius Bonar, 1855
'This is the hour of banquet and of song;
This is the heavenly table spread for me:
Here let me feast, and, feasting, still prolong
  The brief, bright hour of fellowship with thee.'

Lord, we cannot see you with our eyes.
> You are the invisible God and yet you are present.
> You have made yourself known,
> You have given us a revelation of yourself in the things that you have made,
> And we trace your hand in the unfolding of earth's history.

You have spoken to us through your Word.
> And into so many hearts
> —hearts once closed against you.
> You have come in sovereign grace and opened those hearts;
>> We have turned to you,
>> confessed to you our sin,
>> received your forgiveness,
>> and we are now united to our Lord Jesus Christ, and day by day we have communion with him.

We confess that there is nothing like communing with you, gracious God.
> There is none on earth that our hearts desire besides you.
> We pray that you will come near to us again and refresh us.

We can sing the words of this hymn* and it is indeed the expression of the hearts of your people, the longing for renewed, constant, and indeed, unbroken, fellowship with you.
> We thank you for the atoning blood,
> For the propitiation of our sins,

50

And for the reconciliation received.
We thank you for redemption from the curse of
the law and the power of sin.
We thank you for all the rich, varied, and eternal
blessings that have come to us so freely through
Christ and his cross.

We pray that where the knowledge of this great
Saviour—so precious to many of us—is yet unknown, it
would please you to send that knowledge, that into the
dark places of the earth the light of the glorious gospel of
Jesus Christ would shine, and that there, Satan would be
deprived of his power to darken, defile, and destroy.

We thank you for the table of remembrance that is set
before us, and we pray that in the course of our service,

> As we read the Scriptures,
> As we hear them expounded,
> And as we continue to sing,

>> we pray that our hearts would be prepared
>> to come with fresh thankfulness for such a
>> great Saviour and such a great salvation.

We pray that where there are impediments in our hearts
and lives to heartfelt worship and communion with you,
and appreciation of the things of God, that it would
please you in your grace to remove those impediments.

> O God, where there is unconfessed sin and a stain
> upon the conscience,

>> may there be, even now in the quietness of
>> our hearts,
>> confession of that sin,
>> and turning afresh to that Saviour whose
>> blood cleanses from all sin.

> How we thank you for the fountain that has been
> opened for sin and uncleanness!

Lord, where there is doubt, where there are struggles in the areas of faith and assurance,

> We pray that you would come to your beloved people, and clear away those mists;
> May light arise in their darkness,
>> that they might have renewed assurance of the truth of Holy Scripture,
>> of the sure foundation upon which they are building,
>> and of their interest in a Saviour's love.

Where there is sorrow, and where there is heartache, may you come with your gracious Holy Spirit, and pour down your consolation that we may be revived and refreshed this day,

> Able to receive your word,
> To give you worship,
> And to go into the week that stretches before us
>> with our strength renewed,
>> our faith strengthened,
>> and our love towards you, gracious God, enlivened.

Hear us, we pray.

We plead all these things as we commit this whole hour, and indeed, the remainder of this day, into your gracious hands.

We ask it through Jesus Christ our Lord, and for his sake.
Amen.

'Here, O my God, I see thee face to face'

Prayers for Illumination

Prayer for God's Blessing on the Message of the Cross

Isaiah 53:10
'Yet it was the
LORD's will
to crush him
and cause him
to suffer, and
though the
LORD makes
his life a guilt
offering, he
will see his
offspring and
prolong his
days, and the
will of the LORD
will prosper in
his hand.'

Our great and gracious God,
We thank you for the cross of Calvary,
For that cross that stands in human history,
For that place where you, the just and holy God,
made provision at such enormous cost to yourself
for our salvation.

We would come to that cross today in our Scripture
meditation—
We would come with reverence, we would come
with awe ,
We would come with thankful hearts,
And we would come with a most earnest desire
that the message of that cross
would be more fully understood,
more deeply appreciated.

We pray that the blessing that flows from that cross
would flow into each of our lives and especially, we pray,
that it would flow into the lives of those who have not yet
come to know this Christ of Calvary.

Hear us, we pray. Glorify the Son who loved us and gave
himself for us.

We ask it in his precious name.
Amen.

Prayer for Those Preaching God's Word

2 Corinthians 12:9
'But he said to me, "My grace is sufficient for you, for my power is made perfect in weakness."'

Remember, Lord, we pray,
   Those whom you have called this day to preach the Word.
   You know how weak they are in and of themselves,
         but we pray, Lord Jesus,
         that they may know your help as they
         seek to fulfil their part in the Great
         Commission.
   Stand with them;
   Stand with your servant here,
   And may we hear through their lips the Word of the living Christ.

May that Word do amazing things all around the globe.

For your eternal glory we ask it.
Amen.

Prayer for Comfort and Cleansing Through the Preached Word

*Ephesians
5:25b–26*
*'Christ loved
the church and
gave himself
up for her to
make her holy,
cleansing her
by the washing
with water
through the
word.'*

Loving Father,
We ask that as we come to the Holy Scriptures
You would bless to us those Scriptures.
We come to them as sinners,
and we thank you that there is a message of
cleansing
as we come in the consciousness of our
uncleanness.
We thank you for the provision of your love, for a
Saviour whose blood cleanses from all sin.

We pray that as we turn our thoughts to him,
To the cross,
To the perfection of the cleansing that comes
from Calvary,
And to the willingness that is in your heart to
bestow it upon anyone who comes to you in
repentance,
may we be comforted,
and may we know that cleansing as our
own present and personal experience.

Hear us, and bless us, and bless the whole church of
Christ;

Bless the preaching of the Word to the very ends of the
earth, for Jesus' sake.
Amen.

Prayer for Worldwide Spread of the Gospel

Isaiah 9:2
'The people walking in darkness have seen a great light; on those living in the land of the shadow of death a light has dawned.'

L ord,
We ask you so to bless your Word to us now, that
the burden to pray for the worldwide spread of
the gospel would be deepened.

So open our eyes
To the needs of the lost,
To the multitudes that still sit in spiritual
darkness,
And to the glory that will be yours if it pleases you
to save them,
that more and more,
and with ever greater earnestness,
we would make it our prayer that the lost
of all nations would be wonderfully saved.

Hear us and bless your Word to that end, for Jesus' sake.
Amen.

Prayer for Comfort through the Preached Word

O ur great and gracious God,
  We thank you for the Word that is before us
today.
  We pray that it would come as a message from
heaven, full of comfort to each one of us.

For Jesus' sake,
Amen.

Psalm 119:52
'I remember
your ancient
laws, O LORD,
and I find
comfort in
them.'

Prayer for the Holy Spirit's Illumination of the Word

George Atkins, 1819
'All is vain unless the Spirit of the Holy One comes down; Brethren, pray, and holy manna will be showered all around.'

Merciful God,
May it please you to bless to us now your Word
as we read it,
and as we hear it expounded.
May the help of your Holy Spirit be given.

We pray that that Word
would come to our understandings,
and enlighten our understandings.

We pray that it would be a powerful Word that
you would use in our hearts to bring us to faith in
our Lord Jesus Christ.

Hear us, we pray, for his name's sake.
Amen.

Prayer for God's Blessing on the Preached Word

We pray now, Lord Jesus,
  That in your sovereign power
  You would take this Word that speaks of you,
  And bless it to every one of our hearts.

Help us to hear in the voice of the man the voice of our Lord Jesus Christ.

We pray this for your eternal glory.
Amen.

Mary A. Lathbury, 1877

*'Break thou the bread of life, dear Lord, to me,
As thou didst break the loaves beside the sea;
Beyond the sacred page I seek thee, Lord;
My spirit pants for thee, O living Word!'*

Prayer for the Holy Spirit's Ministry in the Midst of Human Weakness

1 Corinthians 2:4–5
'My message and my preaching were not with wise and persuasive words, but with a demonstration of the Spirit's power, so that your faith might not rest on men's wisdom, but on God's power.'

Minister to us, we pray, gracious God, this day according to our needs.

Bless the church in its work and witness to the ends of the earth.
Grant that the strongholds of Satan would be stormed successfully,

that captives would be freed,
that the gospel would do its transforming work in the lives of multitudes and in our life here.

Build your church; sanctify your people through your truth.

Help your servants as they preach your Word this day and as they lead your people in worship.
Grant, Lord, your blessing now as we turn to the portion of Scripture that is before us.
We pray that though preached in human weakness,

this message may come to our hearts with the freshness and power of the blessedly present and active Holy Spirit, for whose ministry we give you thanks,

Through Jesus Christ our Lord,
Amen.

Prayer for the Holy Sprit's Ministry of Illumination and Salvation

Clara H. Scott, 1895
'Silently now I wait for thee, Ready my God, thy will to see, Open my eyes, illumine me, Spirit divine!'

Lord Jesus,
    We thank you for the Holy Scriptures.
We thank you for the Spirit's ministry in giving to us those Scriptures, and for his ministry in illumining our minds as we study them.

We pray for the Spirit's ministry now.
        May he come, and help the one who
        speaks,
        and help us as we listen.
        Help us to understand.

We pray, above all,
        that he would so work in the hearts of
        those who are not yet saved
        that they may be born again—that they
        may be brought into living union with the
        Lord Jesus Christ—that they would be
        cleansed from their sin—even this day.

Amen.

Prayer For the Holy Spirit's Teaching Through the Word

L ord,
We pray that as you have spoken to our hearts in the past,
You would speak to our hearts again today.

Holy Spirit, come!
Without you we can do nothing.
Take the Word; make it powerfully instrumental in your hands to change our lives and to draw us to the Lord Jesus Christ.

Teach us most effectually, we pray, for our Saviour's sake.
Amen.

John 14:26
'But the Counsellor, the Holy Spirit, whom the Father will send in my name, will teach you all things and will remind you of everything I have said to you.'

Prayers of Application

Prayer Following the Gospel Message

James Montgomery, 1823

'O Spirit of the Lord, prepare All the round earth her God to meet; Breathe thou abroad like morning air, Till hearts of stone begin to beat.'

Our great and gracious God,
We thank you that you have given to us an
almighty Saviour,
> One who is Lord and Christ,
> Sovereign and Deliverer.

Help us to believe the truth,
And help us to respond appropriately to that truth
> by submitting our lives unreservedly to his
> lordship,
> and receiving from his loving hand the gift
> of salvation that even now he lovingly
> extends to us.
May no one remain in unbelief, in darkness.
May no one here remain a rebel and a rejecter of
offered grace.

So work, Holy Spirit, as you worked on the Day of
Pentecost,
> That some here may do the very thing that those
> thousands did back then,
> And receive him.

We ask it for his glory's sake.
Amen.

Prayer for God's Grace

W̲e thank you, our great and gracious God,
  For the provisions of the gospel;
  For your beloved Son, our Lord Jesus Christ;
  For the blood that cleanses from all sin;
  For the fountain that has been opened for sin and
  uncleanness.

Give us grace that we might wash and be cleansed:
    That we might come to him in all our filthiness—
    And be robed in the beautiful robe of his spotless,
    stainless righteousness—
    Be acquitted and stand before you justified—
    And know the Holy Spirit work in the very depth
    of our being to make us inwardly clean.

Lord, we pray, that you will so work in the hearts of our
children, our young people, and those adults here who
are not yet saved—
    That they will not harden their hearts against this
    appeal,
    But will come as you have invited.

We ask it for Jesus' sake.
Amen.

Mary Anne S.
Deck, 1813–
1902
'Saviour, I
come to thee;
O Lamb of
God, I pray,
Cleanse me and
save me,
Cleanse me and
save me,
Wash all my
sins away.'

Prayer for Zion, City of our God

Psalm 51:18
'*In your good
pleasure make
Zion prosper;
build up
the walls of
Jerusalem.*'

L ord, in your good pleasure,
   Prosper us,
   Build up our walls,
   Make us strong in the face of all our spiritual
   adversaries,
         that in your strength we may triumph over
         them,
         and that we might be that glorious city
         of God
         —that place of the dwelling of God into
         which others come,
         see you,
         and are drawn to you.

For your name's sake we pray.
Amen.

Prayer for Pardoning Grace to Extend to Others

Psalm 51:13
'Then I will teach transgressors your ways, and sinners will turn back to you.'

Our great and gracious God, we thank you that you are a pardoning God.

May we know that in our own experience,
and then be able, by your grace, to share that
experience with others, that they, too, may turn
back to you.

Bless us as a church,
And do not let, we pray, our sins and
shortcomings damage the body of Christ.

For Jesus' sake, we pray.
Amen.

Prayers of Intercession

The Mystery of Providence

Psalm 130:5
'I wait for the
LORD, my soul
waits, and in
his word I put
my hope.'

We would remember before you, gracious God,
  Those who are struggling this day with the
mystery of your providence,
  Who are perplexed because of the things that have
befallen them,
  Things that they know you have ordained for
them.

Were we to see with your eyes and know with
your thoughts, how profoundly at rest we would
be! But we are finite creatures and our faith is
often weak and when the darkness closes in
around us, how easily we can lose our way,
and find ourselves a prey to all kinds of fears,
perplexities, and doubts.

Have compassion, we pray, upon your people and
strengthen their faith.
  You know those who are grappling with the
  mystery of sickness,
        those that are grappling with the sorrow of
        death,
        others facing fresh outbursts of
        persecution,
        yet others coping with financial loss,
        and problems in their family,
        with the mystery of unanswered prayer,
        and so we could go on.

How we thank you that your great, generous, and
all-loving heart goes out to every one of your people,
the whole world over with a depth and richness and
perfection of understanding that we cannot fathom.

We thank you for the assurances of your Word,
   For the solid foundation for our faith that is given
   to us in the revelation there
      of your character,
      your purposes,
      your promises,
      and your ways.

Give your people grace to wait for you—
   To rest quietly in yourself—
   To be assured that all things work together for
   good to those who love you—
      that you are the God who does all things
      well, and that when your purposes are
      consummated, and we see the end from the
      beginning, we will be able to say from our
      hearts, 'You have done all things well.'

Through Jesus Christ our Lord.
Amen.

Prayer for Faith in the Midst of Suffering

L oving Father,
Teach us what we so much need you to teach us—
to look at all of your dealings with us in the light
of your Calvary love.

Your providences in our lives are often a mystery to us,
and you ordain so many things for your people that are
hard to bear;
There is sickness,
There is sorrow,
There is the pain of betrayal,
And there is sin that mars our churches, our
homes, and our personal lives.
There is war,
There is famine,
And there is much that touches your people,
That makes them wonder at times how this can
consist with the love of God.

We pray that you will strengthen our faith—that we
may see these things in the light of the giving up of your
beloved Son to the cross of Calvary that we might have
our sins forgiven, and have eternal life in your presence.

We know that in the light of such love there is nothing
that is not consistent with that love, and if we will but
wait and trust you, all will be made plain, and we will see
that you are a God who does all things well.

Remember, we pray, those who are in special need at this
time.

*Romans
8:38–39*
*'For I am
convinced
that neither
death nor life,
neither angels
nor demons,
neither the
present nor the
future,
nor any
powers, neither
height nor
depth, nor
anything else
in all creation,
will be able
to separate us
from the love
of God that is
in Christ Jesus
our Lord.'*

We pray for those among us who are sick, for
their healing and for their comfort.
You know every burden that we carry upon our
hearts;

> We would ask that you would strengthen
> us with the knowledge that it is a loving
> God who has ordained these things for us,
> and you will make them to work together
> for our eternal good.

Hear us and bless us for Jesus' sake.
Amen.

Prayer for the Needs of a Fallen World

Psalm 130:1–2
'Out of the depths I cry to you, O LORD; O Lord, hear my voice. Let your ears be attentive to my cry for mercy.'

Merciful God,
We pray for those who are in the depths
And especially for those who are in the depths of their own sin.

We pray that you will enable them to cry out to you for mercy and forgiveness.
How true it is that,
    if you record our sins,
    if you mark them and call us to account for them,
    who shall stand?
But with you there is forgiveness that you may be feared.

We pray that those who are conscious of their guilt today may come to experience that great reality that with you there is forgiveness, and that through the blood of Jesus Christ shed for us on Calvary, that forgiveness may be theirs.

We pray, Father, for others who are in need today;
    We remember those who are sick and pray for their healing.
    We pray for those who are out of work that it would please you, Lord, to provide work for them, and in the meantime to supply every need that they have, and to keep them in your peace.

We pray for the protection of our military in places of conflict.
    We ask you will watch over them,
        safeguard them,

and keep in your peace the many anxious
hearts here in this country as they are
concerned very naturally for the protection
of their loved ones.

We pray for the persecuted,
    For the hungry,
    And for those who are in the darkness of false
    religion;

We pray, Lord,
    for your protection,
    for your gracious supply,
    and for your deliverance.

We pray for those, O God, whom sin has mercilessly in
its grip, those who are slaves of addiction of one kind or
another.
    We pray that you will come,
    and, in your great mercy, break the chains that
    bind them,
    and grant to them that liberty that Jesus Christ
    has come into the world to bring.

We pray for the wrongfully imprisoned,
    That justice would be done,
    That they would be released.

We pray for the rightfully imprisoned,
    And ask, Lord, that you would bless all of the
    agencies that are at work to bring the light of the
    gospel to such.

We pray that the ministry of the Word may bring light
and life
    To those who are in that very difficult situation.
    Bring them face to face with their spiritual need,

and use the ministries of Bible-believing
Christians to bring them to true faith in Jesus
Christ.

Father, we could pray on and on,
for the needs of this fallen world are so many and
so great,
and yet you are the Almighty One.
You are Lord of heaven and earth,
and you are merciful and compassionate.

We pray that you will hear our prayers for those whom
we have mentioned, and that you will hear the prayers of
our heart for many others that cannot be mentioned.

We pray that this day, this Lord's Day, would be a day of
special blessing all around the world, and that you would
show yourself in the midst of all of the ruinous effects of
the Fall as a God who has come in mercy and in love to
change things for the better.

Hear us, we pray, for Jesus' name's sake.
Amen.

Prayer for the Salvation of our Children

Titus 3:4–5a
'But when the kindness and love of God our Saviour appeared, he saved us, not because of righteous things we had done, but because of his mercy.'

Father in heaven,
>We would glorify you for you are the one who gives faith,
>You are the one who brings our faith on, and makes it truly saving faith.
>>We pray that that may be the faith that each one of us has here.

Bless our children.

We thank you for all that they already know and believe,
>For all that they have already experienced of the Lord's kindness.

We pray, Lord,
>That these things would be just so many steps by which you lead them to that faith that draws them to the Saviour, that he might be their Saviour and their King.

Lord, grant it so, we pray, for his name's sake.
Amen.

Prayer for Burdened Hearts

1 Peter 5:7b
'He cares for you.'

L ord,
  We pray for your blessing upon our own work
  here,
  And we thank you for the many opportunities
  that are ours.

  We pray that your blessing would be upon all the
  teaching and proclamation—
          that it would be blessed to those that are
          already saved,
          and would come with saving power to
          those that are not.

We remember, Lord, those who are in special need.
        You know there are many situations that are upon
        our hearts that concern us.
        You know the sadness that is in hearts because of
                concerns that parents have over children,
                children over parents.

You know where there is anxiety because of work
situations.
        We come to you as always as a burdened people.
        We pray that you will minister to us
        And that we will have grace to cast all our cares
        upon you.

We pray that your blessing would be upon us as we come
to your Word.

We thank you for that Word and pray that it may
come to every heart
—every heart—
with power this day.

We implore the aid of the Spirit to that end, and we look
to you to do great things in fulfilment of your purpose.

Through Jesus Christ our Lord we ask these things.
Amen.

Prayer for God's Mercy

*Ephesians
2:4–5*
*'But because
of his great
love for us,
God, who is
rich in mercy,
made us alive
with Christ
even when
we were dead
in transgres-
sions—it is by
grace you have
been saved.'*

Our great and gracious God,
We thank you that no one need despair of your
mercy.
We thank you for the perfect sufficiency of the
atonement made by our Lord and Saviour Jesus
Christ.

We thank you that it is his blood that cleanses from all sin,
And that he is able to save completely all who
come to you by him.
And we pray that those who are troubled with a
sense of their sin,
And who perhaps fear that there is no love in your
heart for them,
We pray that they may be sovereignly and
graciously drawn to the Saviour, and may
experience, this very day, the blessedness
of having their sins forgiven.

We pray, too, for the many who have no concern
for their souls, that it would please you to send the
Holy Spirit to awaken them,
to show them their need,
to bring them face to face with the reality
of what they are in the sight of God,
and of the need that is theirs to come in
lowly penitence to our Lord Jesus Christ.

We pray that we who, by grace, have had our
hearts opened to the Lord Jesus Christ and his love,
that we, this day, and all our days,
would enjoy an ever deeper fellowship
with him.

We thank you for that mysterious and wonderful union
that there is between the Saviour and his people;

    And we pray, Lord Jesus, that by virtue of that
    mysterious and wonderful contact that you have
    with our souls,

        You would mould our wills to your own will;
        That you would grant to us the same mind
        that you have
        that we may think as you think,
        look at everything from your perspective;
        and that you would so influence our
        emotions that the love, the joy, and the
        peace that are in your heart, would be in
        ours also.

We ask it for your glory's sake.
Amen.

Offertory Prayer

1 Peter 4:10
'Each one
should use
whatever gift
he has received
to serve others,
faithfully
administering
God's grace
in its various
forms.'

Lord, as we give,
We are reminded of the privilege that is ours to
play a part in the unfolding drama of redemption.

We thank you that there is no believer who is
useless.
We thank you that each one of us has a part to
play.
You have given to each one of us gifts and you
have given to each one of us opportunities—
we can speak,
we can pray,
and we can so let our light shine
that men will see our good deeds and
glorify our Father in heaven.

We thank you that there is so much that you can do with
the little that we feel that we can do.
We think of that little boy with his few loaves and fish,
And how our Lord Jesus Christ took that little
that he had to give,
And with it fed five thousand and more.
We would do what we can, though it should seem
to be so little in our own eyes.

Help us, we pray, to lay hold of every opportunity to
speak to others about our Saviour,
To take a stand for truth and righteousness,
To comfort our fellow believers,
To bear one another's burdens,
To visit the sick,
To care for the lonely,
To pray for the world and for the church,
for surely, as your Word assures us, our
labour in the Lord is not in vain.

How we thank you that as we endeavour with our gifts
and opportunities to serve the Lord, we are not left to get
on with things on our own. How miserably we would
fail if that were so!

We thank you for the promise in your Word,
      Of the assurance of the Saviour's presence with
      his people to the very end of the age.

We worship you, Lord Jesus, the One constantly with
your people.
      You are the One equipping us;
      The One strengthening us;
      The One giving us wisdom and courage;
      The One making us a blessing to our brothers and
      sisters in the Lord;
      The One making our witness to the lost effective;
      And you are pleased to hear our prayers.

Draw near to every one of us.

Again we pray that we may know that you are here
      To comfort us in our sorrows,
      To enable us to bear our burdens,
      To serve you effectively,
      To bring glory to you in the world,
            and to be the instruments in your hands
            for the advancement of your cause, and the
            glorious unfolding of your purposes.

For your eternal glory we ask it.
Amen.

Prayer for Godly Leaders

William Walsham How, 1871

'The powers ordained by thee with heavenly wisdom bless; May they thy servants be, and rule in righteousness: O Lord, stretch forth thy mighty hand, And guard and bless our fatherland.'

Our great and gracious God,
We pray that you will give us leaders who fear your name. We ask for those who are in authority over us
> that they may be men and women of Christian integrity,
> men and women imbued with the principles of the Word of God, who will themselves walk in your ways and set an example in public office.
We ask, Lord, that you will not give us up to the sway of those who care nothing for you and for your laws.

Give us godly leaders, we pray.

We pray, too, for godly leaders within the church.

We pray for the reformation of the visible church and for great revival within its midst. May those who are in the positions of leadership manifest the same qualities that we see manifest supremely in our Lord Jesus Christ, and that, under the leadership of such men, your church would flourish.

Give us all grace, we pray,
> Everyone who is a member of this congregation or of another congregation, to be a good and faithful servant of Jesus Christ, each one of us. We pray that you will bless our time together to that end.

We pray that you will stand with your servant as he opens up the Word,

That you will put words in his mouth,
That you will give to us illumined minds and
hearts,

> and we pray that you will make that Word
> written upon our hearts,
> and make our time together to be truly a
> means of grace,
> that we, in this week that is before us, may
> walk in your ways.

Hear us, O God, we pray, and these prayers and the
many others that in the silence of our hearts we would
lift to you, the omniscient God.

Hear us, for Jesus' sake.
Amen.

Prayer to Jesus Christ, Sovereign of the World and Head of the Church

Ephesians
1:22
'And God placed all things under his feet and appointed him to be head over everything for the church.'

Almighty God, ever-faithful One,
    We thank you, that in fulfilment of these promises of Scripture,* our Lord Jesus Christ was raised from the dead, and exalted to your right hand. We worship him as the One who is upon the throne of heaven, the One who rules over all.

We pray to you, Lord Jesus, in your headship over the world, that you will bring peace to those parts of our world that are troubled with war and strife.
        We pray that in the exercise of your kind sovereignty, you will provide for the peoples of our world who are in need.
        We pray for those that are in spiritual darkness, that you would send the gospel to them.

We ask you to overrule in the appointment of national leaders in this country and in other countries facing elections, and we ask that in the exercise of your sovereignty, you would help those who already possess authority to govern the nation well.

We pray to you, too, in your headship over the church—
        We thank you for that blessed headship that you exercise over your beloved people—
        We pray that you will encourage and protect your church as a whole and all its individual members.

Minister, we pray,
>to the burdened, the sorrowful,
>the fearful, and the downcast.

We pray that you will strengthen your people's faith.
>Grant to them a deep and unshakeable assurance
>that the One who has all things in his hand has a
>heart of full of love and is infinitely wise.

We pray this for your eternal glory.
Amen.

Acts 2:22–36

Prayer for Persecuted Believers

Our Father in heaven,
Our hearts go out to the people of God in different
parts of the world who are experiencing the most
ferocious and violent persecution.
We pray that you will protect them.
We pray that you will help them not to envy the
arrogant and the wicked.
We pray that you will help them to look to the
end—to see the reward that will be theirs, and not
to envy any wicked man or woman.
Comfort them, we pray.

Comfort any here who may be struggling because of the
opposition and hostility and mockery of worldly men
and women who despise their Christian faith and their
Christian standards.
Help them, we pray, to persevere in their faith and
in their obedience, and to turn a deaf ear to the
things that are said against them.

We do implore you, O God, to work in mighty grace in
the lives of those who are perhaps holding back because
of the price that they know they will have to pay.
Help them to see that this is nothing in
comparison with the blessing that you will pour
into their lives if they will but turn to you in faith
and repentance.

Do bless to us your Word.

We thank you for the privilege of being part of the
church of Jesus Christ.
Thank you for 'the church's one foundation…
Jesus Christ her Lord.'
We thank you for the church's

preservation, for the church's ultimate triumph. Thank you that nothing that Satan can unleash against it can ever thwart your purposes for the church! We pray that it will go on to conquer and to do great exploits.

Build your church, Lord Jesus, we pray, and make it strong and glorious
> in this community,
> in this land,
> and to the ends of the earth.

We ask it for your glory's sake.
Amen.

Prayer for Promised Provision

Philippians
4:19
'And my God
will meet all
your needs
according to
his glorious
riches in Christ
Jesus.'

Father,
We thank you for your provision for the people of
Israel, for the way in which you supplied them
with manna from heaven,
with water from the rock.

You never failed them,
and though they distrusted you,
you proved yourself to be a kind and
faithful God all through those desert
wanderings.

We pray that you will provide for your people who are in
need today.
We ask indeed that you would provide for all
people on the face of the earth, but we pray
especially for those who are praying,
who are looking to you for your provision,
who are seeking to rely upon the promises
of Holy Scripture.

We pray that you will hear their prayers,
that you will come to their aid,
that you will supply their needs,
and in the meantime keep them in
that peace of yours that surpasses all
understanding.

We pray that you will hear us, O God,
for all who are sick,
that it would please you to raise them up.

We pray indeed for all who are upon our hearts, that you
will supply them with what they need. You know those
who are in need of wisdom,

Those who are in need of protection,
Those who need courage,
And those who need your guidance.
You know those who need your salvation.

Hear us, our great and gracious God, as we plead with
you, that out of the infinite fulness that is yours of
wisdom, love, power, and faithfulness,
You would hear our prayers,
Supply those needs,
Bring glory to yourself,
Joy to the hearts of your people,
And salvation to the hearts and lives of the lost.

For your eternal glory we pray.
Amen.

Prayer at the Ordination of Church Officers

Thomas E. Powell, 1864
'*Blest Spirit, in their hearts abide, And give them grace to watch and pray; That, as they seek thy flock to guide, Themselves may keep the narrow way.*'

Our gracious God, with all our hearts we bless you for these men.

We worship you, Lord Jesus, the Head of the church.

We recognize you as the One who gave these men to the church.

Thank you for the call that has been confirmed through the election of the membership, and it is now our joy to set these men apart for the office of elder and deacon.

> Lord, you know the nature in which they must serve and the limitations that are theirs;
>
> We implore for them grace to be good and godly men,
>
> full of the Holy Spirit,
>
> strong in the Lord and in the power of your might,
>
> clothing themselves with the full armour of God,
>
> invested by the Holy Spirit with all needful gifts for this work.

We bless you for these elders.

> We ask that you will help them as they give themselves to the pastoral care of this congregation. Give to them pastoral hearts and pastoral wisdom and may they play their part along with the other shepherds in shepherding this flock.

We thank you for these deacons.

> We pray that you will help them as they give
> themselves to the diaconal work of this church.

>> Again we pray that you will strengthen
>> them as they, too, must serve in fallen
>> human nature and with all their
>> limitations.

We thank you for the gifts of which you have given and
invested all of these men, and we pray that through the
aid of the Spirit, these gifts may be exercised

> To the glory of God,
> To the advancement of the kingdom here,
> And to the very ends of the earth.

We ask these things in Jesus' name.
Amen.

Pastoral Prayer at Beginning of the School Year

Dorothy A. Thrupp, 1836
'*Early let us seek thy favour, early let us do thy will; Blessed Lord and only Saviour, with thy love our bosoms fill: Blessed Jesus, Blessed Jesus, thou hast loved us, love us still.*'

Lord Jesus,
>With all our hearts we would give you thanks for the gift of the Holy Spirit.
>We thank you that he was poured out on the Day of Pentecost and that he remains in the church in the hearts of all the believers.

We thank you for his ministry to your body, the church;
>We thank you for his ministry in the world
>>as he brings conviction of sin,
>>imparts new life,
>>and joins men and women, boys and girls,
>>to yourself.

We pray that he would work very powerfully in the hearts of our children and young people as they begin their classes in our Christian school.
>We pray that this new year that is about to begin in your goodness would be one that is crowned with blessing.

>Be merciful to each of our students and remember those who will teach them.

>We thank you for their labours and pray that they would be encouraged and see much fruit from their work.

Remember, too, we pray,
>Those of our young people who will be attending public school this year;
>We pray that you would protect them from harm.
>We pray that you will help them to choose their friends wisely;

We pray that if they are believers they will be a good witness among their fellow students in the classrooms and to their teachers.

We pray that if they are not yet believers that it would please you to hear the prayers of parents as even now they pour out their hearts to you for the salvation of their loved ones.

We pray for young people in our church that are home-schooled.

> We ask that you will bless the endeavours of their parents, that the minds of these young people will be shaped and moulded by the Word of God.

Remember those who are going off to university.

> We ask that you will watch over them and keep them safe;
>
>> Preserve them in the midst of temptation, and help them to be faithful to you.
>> Help them, we pray, to believe in the Lord Jesus Christ and be saved, if they have not already done so.

For your glory's sake, we pray.
Amen.

Prayer Looking Foward ...

Henry F. Lyte,
1847
'Change and
decay in all
around I see;
O thou who
changest not,
abide with me.'

We worship you,
Our gracious God, as the One who does not
change.

We change, and we will go on changing,
And at last we will come to the end of our lives,
And we will experience the great change.
But all through you are the same;
Your compassions fail not,
Your covenant is never broken,
And you remain eternally committed to
your people.
As you have carried us thus far, so you will
continue to do until the very end.

We pray for those here who are not yet believers, that
they may come, even this day, to Christ.
We ask, Lord, that those of us who are your
people—and especially those who are older and
further down the road—that they will take the
comfort of this text * to heart, and be assured that,
whatever this coming year holds for them, you
will hold them in your almighty and most loving
hand.

Hear us, we pray, for Jesus' sake.
Amen.

'My times are in your hand.' Psalm 31:15a

Prayer at the Closing of Another Year

Matthew 28:20b
'*And surely I am with you always, to the very end of the age.*'

Our great and gracious God,
As we come to the close of another year, we would indeed make it the prayer of our hearts that you would abide with us.

We thank you that you have been with us all through the days of this past year.
Perhaps many a day we have not felt you near,
Perhaps at times we have even felt that you have forsaken us and forgotten us but we thank you that it has never been so.

We thank you that you are constantly with your people, and you have enabled us to persevere in grace,
You have comforted our hearts,
You have heard our prayers,
You have come so often to our aid.

We pray that you will go with us into this new year.
There is none of us who knows what the new year will hold, but we thank you that every moment of that year is in your hands, and you will be with your people.

We thank you that with that promise girding us, we can go forward with confidence and in your peace. We pray that you will help us to walk with you in this new year better than we have ever done before.

Forgive us, Lord, for our sins and our backslidings of this past year.
Grant to us, as the days of the new year unfold, an ever closer walk with you.
Help us to put sin to death,

101

Help us to gladly yield our lives
unreservedly to Jesus Christ, our Saviour
and God, that we may regard ourselves
entirely at his disposal to be, to go, to do,
as he would wish.

We pray that it may be our privilege to serve him,
to bring glory to him,
to help others to know him better,
and to help some, indeed, to come to know
him for the first time.

Have mercy, we pray, upon those connected with us
who come to the end of this year and their hearts are still
closed against you, still hardening their hearts against
you.
Spare them, O God, we pray; spare them!
Grant that this new year would mark the
beginning of new life in Jesus Christ.
We are so thankful for the almighty Holy Spirit,
for his limitless power
to bring conviction of sin,
to give new birth,
and to draw those who are away from you
to faith and to repentance.

We pray, Lord, that you would do that in the
hearts and lives of all who are upon our hearts,

For Jesus' sake,
Amen.

Benedictions

Part us in your peace, and with your grace and mercy resting upon us,

> Supplying every need that we have, that in whatever sphere of life we are called to live and serve,
>> we might glorify you,
>> now and always.

In Jesus Christ our Lord,
Amen.

We give you thanks for this time together, and we pray that we may go from this place in the comfort of what you have done, and what you will yet do, and in the supreme comfort of who you are, our great unchanging God.

> Bless us, and keep us,
> And make your face to shine upon us,
> And be gracious unto us this day and all our days,

Through Jesus Christ our Lord,
Amen.

Gracious God,
    May your rich blessing be upon us through this
    day, and through all our coming days.

May we know your grace,
       your mercy,
       and your peace,
resting upon and abiding with us all, both now
and for evermore.

Amen.

2 John 3
'Grace, mercy
and peace from
God the Father
and from Jesus
Christ, the
Father's Son,
will be with us
in truth and
love.'

Part us with your blessing, we pray.
    Give to each of us that portion of that grace that
    you see we have need to cleanse and to keep us.

For our Saviour's sake,
Amen.

*Julia H.
Johnston*
'Grace, grace,
God's grace,
grace that will
pardon and
cleanse within;
Grace, grace,
God's grace,
grace that is
greater than all
our sin.'

G racious God,
May your blessing be upon us,
blessings of your great salvation through
Jesus Christ.

May they be our portion in ever increasing
measure, now and always.

Through Jesus Christ our Lord,
Amen.

Ephesians 1:3
'Praise be to
the God and
Father of our
Lord Jesus
Christ, who
has blessed us
in the heavenly
realms with
every spiritual
blessing in
Christ.'

W e thank you, gracious God,
For this hour together, and pray for your blessing
to be upon us as we part.

Grant that each one of us may go from this place
with a true and saving faith in our Lord Jesus
Christ.

For his name's sake,
Amen.

John Fawcett,
1773
'Thanks
we give and
adoration for
thy gospel's
joyful sound:
May the fruits
of thy salvation
in our hearts
and lives
abound:
Ever faithful,
Ever faithful to
the truth may
we be found.'

ABOUT DAY ONE:

Day One's threefold commitment:
- To be faithful to the Bible, God's inerrant, infallible Word;
- To be relevant to our modern generation;
- To be excellent in our publication standards.

I continue to be thankful for the publications of Day One. They are biblical; they have sound theology; and they are relevant to the issues at hand. The material is condensed and manageable while, at the same time, being complete—a challenging balance to find. We are happy in our ministry to make use of these excellent publications.

JOHN MACARTHUR, PASTOR-TEACHER, GRACE COMMUNITY CHURCH, CALIFORNIA

It is a great encouragement to see Day One making such excellent progress. Their publications are always biblical, accessible and attractively produced, with no compromise on quality. Long may their progress continue and increase!

JOHN BLANCHARD, AUTHOR, EVANGELIST AND APOLOGIST

Visit our web site for more information and
to request a free catalogue of our books.
www.dayone.co.uk

U.S. web site:
www.dayonebookstore.com

Also available

When Heaven calls your name

People in the Bible who heard God speak

ROGER ELLSWORTH

128PP, PAPERBACK

ISBN 978-1-84625-102-3

Believing that repetition indicates emphasis, Roger Ellsworth examines occasions in the Bible in which God the Father or God the Son repeated someone's name. He asserts that these instances were meant to make certain truths 'dance' before our eyes. In an increasingly difficult and challenging world, these truths will thrill, comfort and guide all those who genuinely embrace them.

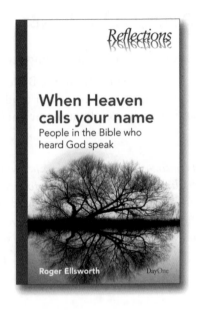

'God speaks. He has spoken, and he continues to speak today. Through these vivid portraits of Heaven's calls, you will overhear the voice of God speaking specifically and clearly to you.'

TODD BRADY, PASTOR OF THE FIRST BAPTIST CHURCH OF PADUCAH, KENTUCKY, USA

'Roger Ellsworth has given us another book full of pastoral integrity and fidelity to the Word of God. *When Heaven calls your name* is both exegetically sound and devotionally warm—a book that is as heart-stirring as it is instructional. The readers of this book who hear their names called will grow in the faith and knowledge of our Lord and Saviour, Jesus Christ. I heartily recommend it!'

IVAN SCHOEN, PASTOR, MARANATHA BAPTIST CHURCH, POPLAR GROVE, ILLINOIS, USA

Also available

Under God's smile
The Trinitarian Blessing of
2 Corinthians 13:14

DEREK PRIME

128PP, PAPERBACK

ISBN 978-1-84625-059-0

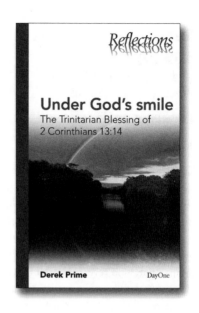

During recent decades, it has become the practice of Christians in many churches and in university and college Christian Unions to commit one another to God's grace and care with the words 'May the grace of the Lord Jesus Christ, and the love of God, and the fellowship of the Holy Spirit be with us all' (2 Corinthians 13:14). They are familiar words, but what do they actually mean? For what are we praying?

So that we do not repeat these words without appreciating their full implication, Derek Prime explores them and considers the three Persons of the Trinity in their different, yet perfectly harmonious, relationship to every believer. Written in an easy-to-read style, this book is thoroughly rooted in the Scriptures and is a demonstration that solid biblical truth is both heart-warming and exciting.

'An easily-read book, helpful in all stages of Christian life.'
GRACE MAGAZINE

'Derek Prime's ministry is much appreciated by many Christian groups, including ourselves. Like all his other books … biblically based and easy to read.'
ASSOCIATED PRESBYTERIANS NEWS

'If, like me, you are constantly on the lookout for books that say a great deal in short order, you will be delighted by what you hold in your hand. It is a special gift not only to expound what the blessing of the triune God means, but also to explain why it matters. We have come to expect this from Derek Prime, and once again he hits the mark.'
ALISTAIR BEGG, SENIOR PASTOR, PARKSIDE CHURCH, CHAGRIN FALLS, OHIO

Also available

Seasons of comfort and joy
Meditations in verse based on select Scripture readings

ANNE STANDFIELD

96PP, PAPERBACK

ISBN 978-1-84625-103-0

God's Word, the Bible, is the guidebook to life for all people. It is the 'measuring rod' or standard by which we live out our lives before God, the Creator of all things. In it, God reveals himself to us and teaches us about ourselves and the world around us. God's Word is vital in revealing the truth to each of us; only the Bible teaches us how sinful people can ever be reconciled to a holy God.

In these warm, Christ-centred poems, Anne Standfield demonstrates her joy in the truths of God's Word, sharing her experiences of God and the knowledge of his Word with others with a view that they, with her, 'may know him better' (Ephesians 1:17). All the poems have been based solely upon Scripture with the aim that each reader may come to know the only true God and Jesus Christ, his Son, whom he has sent as our Saviour. This is the only way to eternal life (John 17:3).